Little Feelings

Little Feelings

By Judy Spain Barton

Illustrated by
Benjamin Hummel

Prometheus Books
59 John Glenn Drive
Amherst, New York 14228-2197

Published 1998 by Prometheus Books

02 01 00 99 98   5 4 3 2 1

Library of Congress Cataloging-in-Publication Data

Barton, Judy Spain.
    Little feelings/Judy Spain Barton; illustrated by Benjamin Hummel.
        p.   cm.
    Summary: A collection of poems to help readers be more comfortable expressing the wide range of feelings they may encounter in their early years and as they grow, including feeling happy, mad, scared, sad, and just plain alive.
    ISBN 1–57392–183–1 (alk. paper)
    1. Emotions—Juvenile poetry. 2. Children's poetry, American. (1. Emotions—Poetry. 2. American poetry.)
I. Hummel, Benjamin, ill. II. Title.
PS3552.A772L58   1998
811′.54—dc21   97–41720
                                                        CIP
                                                         AC

Printed in the United States of America on acid-free paper

What's in this Book?

Other Stuff

A Note to Parents

Feelings are the essence of our being. They mold and shape who we are. How they are explored and understood in early childhood is vital to the adult we become.

Bonding and sound parent-child relationships are formed from feelings that are openly shared, and promote confidence as well as positive self-esteem.

Children are not usually capable of identifying, relating, or sorting their feelings. It is difficult for them to understand and manage feelings they may experience.

Little Feelings has been designed and written to provide young readers with the tools to promote understanding and the confidence to address their feelings.

It is an easy, nonthreatening way for adults to approach these sometimes sensitive issues and assist in this learning process.

Little Feelings allows the child to realize that he or she is okay and that sharing life is the basis for a happy life.

Acknowledgments

Special thanks and love go out to Brett Barton, Benjamin Hummel, Connie Hendrix, Mary Nelson, Barbara and Bill Barton, the children of Synthesis, and the Synthesis staff. All my thanks and love to Paul, Brady, David, Sean, Laurene, Megan, and Andrew.

Little Feelings

Does anyone out there
Really know how I feel?
Is it just 'cause I'm little,
That my feelings can't be real?
Big people laugh;
They get scared and they cry,
They always can tell you
How they feel and just why.
We little ones feel,
We just couldn't explain
What it means when we're happy
Or why we feel pain.
Someone should help us
So life's not so tough.
We'd feel pretty good
If we knew all this stuff!

Just Me

Oh, Happy Me!

Happy, happy, happy,
That's what I like to be.
It doesn't matter where I go,
I take a smile with me.
There's lots of things
That I could say
Would make me feel this way.
Love and friends and family
Keep me smiling every day.
And when I help my mommy out,
By cleaning up my mess,
It makes her smile and give me hugs,
And she tells me I'm the best.
Happy is the greatest,
As everyone should know.
It makes you want to jump and sing,
And gives your face a glow.
I'm glad I can feel happy.
It's fun to feel this way.
I wish for everyone I meet
To feel this way each day!

I'm Mad!

Have you ever been mad,
So mad you could scream?
Your face turns all red,
And your head fills with steam?
When you have to do things
That you don't want to do,
Or your friend breaks a toy
And tries to blame you.
Getting mad is okay,
It's what to do that is tough.
You wouldn't throw fits
Or run off in a huff.
Maybe a walk in the yard,
If you could.
Better yet, talking about it
Would really be good.
Getting mad sometimes happens,
And it doesn't have to be bad.
Getting mad even happens
To your mom and your dad.

Love Is Great!

There's all kinds of love,
It lives everywhere.
You can get it and give it,
It's so fun to share!
You can share it with friends
Or your family, it's true.
You can share it with teachers
Or your favorite pet, too.
Love means a lot
From your mom and your dad,
'Cause they show it each day,
Even if you act bad!
It's easy to show love
With a hug and a kiss,
Or by helping and giving,
Or even granting a wish.
You can make the day happy,
And make smiles happen, too,
With just three little words—
I LOVE YOU!

I'm Scared!

Little kids are scared a lot
Of things that they don't know,
Of shadows in the dark at night,
Of movies and TV shows.
We are scared of lots of things,
It sometimes makes us cry.
It can make our stomachs ache
And make us shake inside.
I wonder if the grown-ups
Get scared a lot like us.
It's hard to see it, if they do,
'Cause they don't make a fuss.
My mommy tells me it's okay,
It gets better and I'll see.
She'll help me through the scary times,
She takes good care of me.
So I guess it's true, when we get big,
That this will go away.
Or maybe that's why Grandma's hair
Has turned from red to gray!

Sad Feelings

Sometimes I feel sad,
And it makes me cry.
At times I feel sad,
And don't even know why.
Being sick is the worst,
Then I need someone near,
Or when Dad is at work
And I wish he was here.
And when Mommy is sad,
Then I feel sad, too.
It's hard, when you're little,
To know what to do.
Sad feels so gloomy,
Like dark rainy days,
And nothing seems good,
Not even to play.
Being sad isn't fun!
I don't like it, you see.
It's really too hard
For little kids like me.

I Hate You!

Hate can be a problem,
It comes with being mad.
It's the maddest you could ever get,
The worst feeling ever had.
It's okay to feel that hate,
And say it, if you must.
But be sure you really mean it
Before raising such a fuss.
To tell someone you hate them
Could make them feel so bad.
They'd feel not loved or wanted,
And might think that they are bad.
Hate is just a feeling,
It's with us, then it's not.
But hate can hurt more in your heart,
And make you cry a lot.
You could talk about the hate you feel,
It's better when you do.
It helps the anger go away
And then the hate will, too.

All by Myself

Some days I feel so all alone.
No matter what I do,
I still feel lost and lonely,
Do you feel that way, too?
It's hard to say just how it feels,
It kind of makes me sad.
Sometimes it's even scary,
And at times it makes me mad.
When I'm just with adults,
And there's no other kids around,
I feel like I am lost in space,
An alien in town.
I don't feel lonely every day,
And for that, I'm really glad.
But at bedtime it is sometimes hard,
And I need my mom or dad.
They say, "You need some time alone,"
I'm not sure I agree.
But maybe when I'm older,
I can be alone, with me.

I'm Okay!

I know me, and I'm really neat!
My mom says I'm the best!
I really am quite special!
I'm not like all the rest.
There's lots of things that I can do,
The best is "being me."
And that's okay, I like that part,
I like who I can be.
I try real hard to be my best,
I don't like acting bad,
But sometimes I can't help it,
And I make my parents mad.
At those times when I act out,
My parents tell me so.
That's how I learn what's right from wrong,
It helps to make me grow.
My parents try to understand
'Cause they were little, too.
They really do still love me
No matter what I do.
As I grow up and learn more stuff,
The better I will be.
I'll be the greatest kid in town
'Cause I'm okay—I'm ME!

In My Life

Just One More Thing!

Just one more thing,
And I think I'll scream!
It's been one of those days—
The WORST, it would seem!
Everything has gone wrong
At home and at school.
My friend even hates me,
He says I'm not cool!
Some days are so hard,
I'd like to just scream,
Or at least hide away
And pretend it's a dream.
But I'll stick it out,
And try it once more,
And hope that tomorrow
Gets better for sure!!

It's All My Fault!!

Have you ever had things happen
That make you feel real bad?
You feel like you did something wrong
But you aren't sure if you have.
You feel like things are all your fault,
But you're much too scared to ask
For fear it would be even worse
Or make someone more mad.
Maybe there's another cause,
Maybe it isn't you.
Knowing sure would ease your mind,
But what are you to do?
All this makes your head feel tight,
It makes you want to cry.
So maybe you should dare to ask,
And then you'd know just why!

Little Kid—Go Away!

They brought a baby home,
"He's cute as he can be."
They say I should be happy
And he looks a lot like me.
Well, all he does is wet and cry
And take all Mommy's time.
He doesn't walk or talk at all
And drinks some awful slime.
Where ever did they get him?
They need to take him back.
It's not that I don't like him,
But I'll gladly help him pack.
Who needs a little brother?
He's much too small to play.
He'll follow me around and stuff
And just get in the way.
But I guess we have to keep him,
So I'll teach him every day
About being a good brother,
Then I guess he'll be okay.

Curious Me

Lots of things happen
And I don't know why.
I don't even know
How birds and planes fly.
I don't know just why
The stars shine at night,
Or who named my hands—
One left and one right.
So I ask my mom "Why?"
And how it can be,
'Cause I want to know all
About all that I see.
The world is a place
To learn about and explore,
To find out the whys,
The hows, and what fors!

They Just Don't Love Me Anymore!

It seems like all they do is fuss
And tell me NO a lot.
There's nothing I can do just right—
A perfect kid, I'm not.
I didn't mean to make a mess,
And the dog got in my way.
The new baby should be woke up,
It's not good to sleep all day.
I guess they just don't love me,
But I used to be their pet.
But now I'm just a problem,
And trouble's what they get.
I don't know how to fix it all.
I try to be real good
But all I do is mess things up,
I'd fix it if I could.
Oh wait—my mommy needs my help?
I guess I'm not that bad!
I even got a great big hug.
A bad day is all they had.

I Just Can't Wait!

Gee, I'm so excited!
Oh boy, I just can't wait!
It feels like I could burst inside,
I'm really in a state.
These times are really hard for me,
I know you understand.
It's like waiting for your birthday
Or Santa's sleigh to land.
It feels like I've got jumping beans
Inside my shoes and clothes.
I must keep on the move
Or I'm sure that I'll explode.
Mom says I should calm myself,
And it's not that I don't try.
But my mind keeps going 'round and 'round,
And I feel like I should fly.
But after all the waiting,
And the time has finally come,
I forget about how hard it was
And have a lot of fun.

I Can Do It Myself!

I can do it myself,
Just watch me and see!
I can put on my clothes
And count way past three.
I can clean up my room
And help rake the yard,
Take care of the dog—
It's really not hard.
Adults think I can't
'Cause I'm too little still.
But I can show them
If they let me, I will.
I don't understand
Why they treat me this way.
There's lots I can do—
Not just "go and play."
I should have a chance,
I'm smart as can be.
I really CAN do it,
If they'd try me and see!

Bored! Bored! Bored!

Golly gee, woe is me,
I'm bored right out of my mind.
What to do? Not even a clue!
There isn't a thing I can find.
I've read all my books,
And my toys aren't much fun.
My mom says to wait,
But she'll never get done.
So, what can I do
When I haven't a clue?
Well, maybe I'll color
A picture or two.
Or maybe I'll write,
I do that pretty good,
Or maybe I'll sing,
Yeah, maybe I could.
I guess if I think about it,
There are things I could do.
Yeah, I'm pretty smart,
I can think of a few.

What Can I Do?

Worrying is like being scared
Of things you think might come,
And of things you think will happen,
When all is said and done.
At times it can seem pretty tough.
There's something you should do.
You wish that you could fix it all,
But how could that be true?
Knowing what to do is hard,
For little kids, it's true.
But sometimes things just go away
With just a hug or two.
Worrying can make you sick,
So it's not too good for you.
It's better if you ask for help
To think the whole thing through.
Grown-ups can be lots of help,
Or maybe a friend could, too,
Talking about it might just work,
And you'd know just what to do.

Other Stuff

Being a Friend

A friend is someone special
And having one is neat.
Being one is extra great
'Cause friends are such a treat.
Friends are fun to talk to
And tell our secrets to,
To share our hopes and dreams with
And everything we do.
Our friends are just like family,
They're there to love and care.
We plan our lives together,
There's nothing we can't share.
We know each other inside out
Like no one else could do.
We learn and play together,
And do silly fun things, too.
Friends are there forever.
We love in special ways.
Even when we're all grown up,
We'll share life every day.

My Family

Family is a special place,
It's where I know I belong.
There's lots of love and comfort there,
A place that's safe from harm.
Families live inside your heart,
It's all that stuff you share—
The happy and the sad things,
and all the love and care.
It's not just moms and dads, you know,
It's anyone you choose.
It's brothers, aunts, and grandpas,
Even friends can be family, too.
So it's not the "who" that really counts,
It's someone whose always there.
Anytime you need them,
They're always there to care.

Being Big

It looks like fun to be grown up—
I wonder if it's true.
They do most anything they want,
And know a whole lot, too.
They eat just when and what they want,
And do hard jobs with ease.
They don't even need permission
To do just what they please.
I just can't wait till I am big.
Oh boy, the things I'll do.
I could even be the president
Or a doctor, if I choose.
My parents say it's hard sometimes,
That being big is tough.
They say there's lots of worries
And other rotten stuff.
I guess I just don't understand
How it could be so rough.
But as a kid I just can't see
'Cause I'm not big enough.

Wants and Wishes

I want and wish a lot each day,
I want all that I see.
I truly want most everything,
And wish that it could be.
I want each toy and ice cream cone.
I wish to own the stores.
I want to do just what I want,
And wish I could do more.
Sometimes my wishes do come true,
And things I want, I get,
But not just if I ask a lot
Or be a silly pest.
The things I want I have to earn,
Like treats for helping out.
But wishes are for always,
It's what kids are all about.

Not Like Me?

Kids are kids I must explain,
A little bit different but mostly the same.
We all start off little and grow to be big,
But we all don't like broccoli or kissing a pig.
We do love our ice cream and goodies to eat.
We don't always like that our room must be neat.
Some of us like dogs and others like cats,
But we all love to play wherever we're at.
Some kids can't do what the rest of us do,
Their bodies don't work right—I wish they could, too.
Our eyes, hair, and skin are all different, you see,
But kids are still kids—we're the same, you and me.
As kids we want all the very same things—
To be safe, loved, and cared for in all that life brings.
We're different a lot as different can be,
But we're all still the same—we're kids, don't you see!

I Dare You!

Some people like to dare you
Or try to make you do
Things you really shouldn't
Or things you don't want to.
Saying NO is hard sometimes,
You're not sure what to do.
You want to still be liked
And do the right thing, too.
Even though they pressure me,
I have to do what's best.
I have to do what's right for me—
Who cares about the rest!
So let the dares keep coming,
I'll take a dare, you see.
I'll dare to be just who I am,
I'll dare to be—JUST ME!

Choices

At times it's hard
To make up my mind.
I'm just not real sure
What to do all the time.
There's too many choices.
Should I do this or do that?
I don't know, I don't know,
I can't think quite that fast.
I am pretty smart,
So I take a deep breath,
Put on my thinking cap,
And do what seems best.
If I choose the wrong thing,
It might really be bad.
But I could choose the best one
And really be glad.
A grown-up could help me,
That's just what I need.
Now that's a smart choice,
I know you'll agree.

My Nighttime World

I live another life through dreams.
My mind works while I sleep,
It thinks about all I have done
And imagines things to be.
There's thoughts of all the good and bad
I see, and say, and do.
It supposes if I wish
That my wishes can come true.
When my mind thinks of the bad things,
Sometimes it's hard to sleep.
It's even sometimes scary,
And I wake and start to weep.
My nighttime thoughts are still okay,
I really shouldn't fret.
There's nothing that will hurt me.
It's just a dream, I'll bet!